THE OFFICIAL
MANCHESTER CITY
ANNUAL 2015

A Grange Publication

© 2014. Published by Grange Communications Ltd., Edinburgh, under licence from Manchester City Football Club. Printed in the EU.

Written by David Clayton

Dedication: For Ben & Gill

Pictures © MCFC (thanks to Sharon Latham)

ISBN: 978-1-908925-68-8

£7.99

Contents

CHAMPIONS AGAIN!

THE STORY OF CITY'S DRAMATIC 2013/14 PREMIER LEAGUE SEASON

AUGUST HEADLINES:

SLICK CITY OFF AND RUNNING!

CITY SWEPT ASIDE ALAN PARDEW'S NEWCASTLE UNITED WITH A PERFORMANCE THAT SUGGESTS THE BLUES WILL TAKE SOME STOPPING THIS SEASON. IN MANUEL PELLEGRINI'S FIRST OFFICIAL GAME IN CHARGE, DAVID SILVA NODDED THE BALL HOME AFTER JUST SIX MINUTES AND SERGIO AGUERO MADE IT 2—0 AFTER 22 MINUTES. FURTHER GOALS FROM YAYA TOURE AND SAMIR NASRI SEALED AN IMPRESSIVE 4—0 VICTORY.

CARDIFF STUN BLUES!

CARDIFF CITY PULLED OFF A SHOCK WIN OVER PELLEGRINI'S CITY WITH THE SOUTH WALES SIDE COMING FROM BEHIND TO SCORE THREE LATE GOALS AND PULL OFF A FAMOUS WIN. WITH THE CARDIFF CITY STADIUM ROCKING, POOR MARKING FROM CORNERS COST CITY – WHO HAD LED THROUGH EDIN DZEKO – DEAR AND ALVARO NEGREDO'S INJURY TIME HEADER PROVED NO MORE THAN A CONSOLATION IN A 3–2 DEFEAT.

SEPTEMBER HEADLINES:

CITY THRASH REDS

CITY MOVED BACK UP TO THIRD IN THE PREMIER LEAGUE WITH A CRUCIAL WIN OVER NEIGHBOURS MANCHESTER UNITED. IN ONE OF THE MOST ONE-SIDED MANCHESTER DERBIES IN YEARS, AGUERO AND YAYA TOURE SCORED BEFORE THE BREAK TO PUT PELLEGRINI'S MEN 2–0 UP AND THEN CITY ADDED TWO MORE IN THE OPENING FIVE MINUTES OF THE SECOND HALF TO LOOK SET TO RUN UP A CRICKET SCORE, BUT THE BLUES DECLARED AT FOUR AND COASTED OUT THE REMAINING MINUTES TO WIN 4–1.

CITY'S POOR AWAY FOR CONTINUES

QUESTION MARKS OVER CITY'S TITLE CREDENTIALS WERE RAISED AGAIN AS ASTON VILLA CAME FROM BEHIND TO SCORE TWICE LATE ON AND SEAL AN EXCITING 3–2. WIN OVER PELLEGRINI'S MEN. LEADING THROUGH YAYA TOURE AND THEN DZEKO'S GOALS, VILLA PRODUCED A STUNNING COMEBACK TO WIN 3–2 TRIPS TO CARDIFF, STOKE AND VILLA PRODUCED JUST ONE POINT FOR THE TITLE-CHASING CITY WHO SLIPPED TO FIFTH.

HAMMER TIME!

CITY ARE BACK ON TRACK AFTER BACK-TO-BACK WINS OVER EVERTON AND WEST HAM. THE BLUES ENDED THEIR AWAY JINX AT UPTON PARK TO SECURE A FIRST WIN OF THE SEASON ON THE ROAD WITH A 3-1 WIN OVER THE HAMMERS. TWO AGUERO GOALS AND ANOTHER FROM SILVA WRAPPED UP AN IMPRESSIVE WIN THAT SEES CITY BACK UP TO FOURTH IN THE TABLE.

NOVEMBER HEADLINES:

SEVENTH HEAVEN FOR CITY!

CITY WERE IN BLISTERING FORM AS THEY PUT NORWICH TO THE SWORD AT THE ETIHAD STADIUM. THE BLUES WERE 4-0 UP WITH JUST 36 MINUTES GONE WITH THE BLOSSOMING PARTNERSHIP OF AGUERO AND NEGREDO CAUSING HAVOC IN THE CANARIES DEFENCE. THEY SCORED TWO OWN GOALS AS PANIC SET IN. CITY ADDED THREE MORE AFTER THE BREAK TO SECURE A 7-0 WIN OVER CHRIS HUGHTON'S SIDE WHO, IN TRUTH, GOT AWAY LIGHTLY ON THE DAY.

CITY MUST IMPROVE ON THE ROAD

STRUGGLING SUNDERLAND PULLED OFF A SHOCK 1-0 WIN AT THE STADIUM OF LIGHT TO FURTHER DENT CITY'S TITLE HOPES. IT WAS THE FOURTH YEAR IN A ROW CITY HAVE LOST BY THE SAME SCORE-LINE AWAY TO THE BLACK CATS AS CITY SLIPPED TO A SEASON LOW OF EIGHTH POSITION IN THE TABLE. CITY KNEW THEY COULD NOT AFFORD ANYMORE SLIP-UPS IF THEY WERE TO STAND ANY CHANCE OF CATCHING THE TEAMS AT THE TOP.

SUPER CITY STUN SPURS

TOTTENHAM LEFT THE ETIHAD STADIUM HAVING BEEN TAUGHT A LESSON IN FINISHING. JESUS NAVAS SCORED WITHIN THE FIRST MINUTE AND THE BLUES WERE 3-0 UP BY THE BREAK. AGUERO, NEGREDO AND ANOTHER NAVAS GOAL COMPLETED THE ROUT AS CITY CONTINUED TO SCORE GOALS FOR FUN AT HOME AND THE WIN PUT CITY BACK UP TO FOURTH IN THE TABLE.

DECEMBER HEADLINES:

BLUES BOX CLEVER

CITY EDGED PAST AN IMPRESSIVE LIVERPOOL SIDE WITH GOALS FROM VINCENT KOMPANY AND NEGREDO ENOUGH TO BEAT LIVERPOOL 2–1. IN A THRILLING BOXING DAY ENCOUNTER, THE REDS MATCHED CITY ALL THE WAY AND LEFT THE ETIHAD WONDERING HOW THEY FAILED TO TAKE HOME AT LEAST A POINT AGAINST A CITY TEAM WHO SURVIVED A NUMBER OF CLOSE SHAVES IN THE SECOND-HALF. ALL THAT MATTERED WAS THE RESULT, HOWEVER, AND WHO KNEW HOW CRUCIAL THAT VICTORY WOULD PROVE TO BE?

JANUARY HEADLINES:

OUT-GUNNED!

IN PERHAPS THE MOST ENTERTAINING GAME OF THE SEASON SO FAR, MANCHESTER CITY AND ARSENAL PRODUCED A NINE-GOAL THRILLER IN A MATCH THAT HAD EVERYTHING. CITY NEEDED TO WIN TO CLOSE THE GAP ON THE GUNNERS AND THE TWO TEAMS WENT HEAD-TO-HEAD IN A MATCH BRIMMING WITH EXCELLENT ATTACKING BUT POOR DEFENDING. ARSENAL SIMPLY COULDN'T COPE WITH CITY'S FIREPOWER AND EVENTUALLY LOST 6–3 AS PELLEGRINI'S SIDE BLEW THE TITLE RACE WIDE OPEN AGAIN.

CITY END JANUARY IN SUBLIME FORM

SPURS MANAGER TIM SHERWOOD CLAIMED CITY WERE 'ON A DIFFERENT PLANET' AFTER SEEING HIS SIDE DISMANTLED AT WHITE HART LANE. FOR THE SECOND TIME IN THREE YEARS, CITY LEFT NORTH LONDON WITH A 5–1 WIN AFTER A STUNNING PERFORMANCE SENT PELLEGRINI'S MEN TO THE TOP OF THE TABLE FOR ONLY THE SECOND TIME THIS SEASON. THE ONLY BLEMISH ON AN OTHERWISE PERFECT EVENING WAS THE LOSS OF SERGIO AGUERO TO INJURY WITH THE ARGENTINE IN BLISTERING FORM.

FEBRUARY HEADLINES:

CITY FAIL CHELSEA TEST

CHELSEA WERE ACCUSED OF 'PARKING THE BUS' AS THEY ENDED MANCHESTER CITY'S PROUD HOME RECORD WITH A 1-0 WIN AT THE ETIHAD STADIUM. JOSE MOURINHO MASTERMINDED A SUPERB DISPLAY AGAINST THE PREMIER LEAGUE LEADERS AND HE DIDN'T CARE ONE JOT ABOUT HIS TACTICS BEING CRITICISED AS THE WEST LONDON SIDE PROVED THEY WERE VERY MUCH IN THE TITLE RACE WHILE RAISING QUESTION-MARKS ABOUT THE BLUES' OWN HOPES OF BECOMING CHAMPIONS.

MARCH HEADLINES:

TEN-MAN CITY SHOW TITLE CLASS

WITH SKIPPER VINCENT KOMPANY SENT OFF IN THE FIRST TEN MINUTES AND CITY REDUCED TO TEN MEN, IT LOOKED AS THOUGH THE BLUES' TITLE HOPES MIGHT TAKE A FATAL BLOW AT THE KC STADIUM BUT CITY DUG IN DEEP AND PRODUCED A SUPERB FIGHTING DISPLAY THAT SUGGESTED PELLEGRINI'S SIDE WOULD FIGHT TO THE END. GOALS IN EACH FROM SILVA AND DZEKO SEALED A MEMORABLE WIN AND THE REACTION AT THE END SUGGESTED CITY HAD THE BELLY FOR THE BATTLE.

REDS HUMBLED

CITY COMPLETED THE DOUBLE OVER MANCHESTER UNITED WITH A COMFORTABLE 3—0 WIN OVER THE REDS AT OLD TRAFFORD. IT WAS CITY'S THIRD SUCCESSIVE WIN AT UNITED AND FROM THE MOMENT DZEKO PUT PELLEGRINI'S SIDE AHEAD INSIDE THE FIRST MINUTE, THE RESULT WAS NEVER IN DOUBT. DZEKO ADDED A SECOND AFTER THE BREAK AND YAYA TOURE SEALED THE WIN IN THE DYING SECONDS TO RUB SALT IN THE WOUNDS OF DAVID MOYES' STRUGGLING SIDE.

APRIL HEADLINES:

LIVERPOOL'S TO LOSE?

CITY KNEW THEY WERE RELYING ON LIVERPOOL TO SLIP UP IF THEY WERE TO HAVE ANY CHANCE OF WINNING THE PREMIER LEAGUE. DESPITE COMING BACK FROM 2—0 DOWN AND GOING WITHIN A WHISKER OF TAKING THE LEAD, CITY CONCEDED A LATE WINNER TO COUTINHO TO SEND ANFIELD CRAZY AND LEFT THE REDS NEEDING TO WIN THEIR FINAL FOUR GAMES TO GUARANTEE THE TITLE.

MORE BLACK CATS WOE

CITY MANAGED TO SALVAGE A DRAW WITH A LATE SAMIR NASRI EQUALISER BUT TWO MORE DROPPED POINTS MEANT CITY KNEW THAT THE TITLE RACE WAS NOW VERY MUCH IN LIVERPOOL'S HANDS. SUNDERLAND PRODUCED AN IMPRESSIVE DISPLAY TO COME FROM BEHIND A LEAD 2—1 WITH JUST MINUTES REMAINING. NASRI MADE IT 2—2 ON 88 MINUTES AND COULD EVEN HAVE WON IT BUT CITY FELL FURTHER BEHIND IN THE RACE TO BE CHAMPIONS AND NOW NEEDED LIVERPOOL TO STUMBLE TWICE IN THEIR REMAINING FOUR MATCHES.

CITY
BACK ON THE HUNT!

LIVERPOOL'S 2–0 DEFEAT AT HOME TO CHELSEA MEANT THE TITLE RACE WAS BACK ON FOR CITY, WHO KNEW OF THE ANFIELD RESULT BEFORE THE MATCH AWAY TO CRYSTAL PALACE AND THE 2–0 WIN AT SELHURST PARK THAT PUT CITY WITHIN THREE POINTS OF THE LEADERS WITH A GAME IN HAND. AN EARLY GOAL FROM DZEKO AND A SECOND FROM YAYA TOURE MEANT, WITH A BETTER GOAL DIFFERENCE, IF CITY COULD WIN THEIR REMAINING THREE GAMES, THEIR SUPERIOR GOAL DIFFERENCE COULD SEE THEM WIN A SECOND TITLE IN THREE YEARS.

CITY WEAR DOWN VILLA TO MOVE CLOSER TO GLORY

FOR 64 LONG MINUTES, NAILS WERE BITTEN, STRESS LEVELS WERE HIGH AND ANXIETY FILLED THE AIR, BUT THEN EDIN DZEKO FINALLY BROKE DOWN A STUBBORN ASTON VILLA DEFENCE TO SEND THE ETIHAD WILD WITH DELIGHT AND RELIEF – AND THE FLOODGATES OPENED. WITH LIVERPOOL THROWING A 3–0 LEAD AWAY AT CRYSTAL PALACE AND CITY SECURING A 3–2 WIN AT EVERTON THE PREVIOUS WEEKEND, CITY'S 4–0 WIN OVER VILLA MEANT PELLEGRINI'S SIDE NOW NEEDED JUST ONE MORE POINT TO WIN A TITLE THAT FOR SO LONG LOOKED TO BE HEADING TO MERSEYSIDE.

CITY ARE CHAMPIONS!

CITY WERE CROWNED PREMIER LEAGUE CHAMPIONS FOR THE SECOND TIME IN THREE YEARS AFTER A 2-0 WIN OVER WEST HAM AT THE ETIHAD STADIUM. THE RESULT WAS NEVER IN ANY DOUBT AS THE BLUES CONTROLLED THE GAME FROM START TO FINISH WITH SAMIR NASRI AND VINCENT KOMPANY SCORING A GOAL IN EACH HALF TO SEAL A SUPERB TURNAROUND IN FORTUNES FROM A TEAM WHO REFUSED TO GIVE UP AND FOUGHT TO THE END.

Top10
Goals of the Season 2013/14

 10 **09** **08** **07** **06**

YAYA V PLZEN 17/09/2013	AGUERO V MAN UNITED 22/09/2013	NEGREDO V TOTTENHAM 24/11/2013	KOLAROV V LEICESTER 17/12/2013	NEGREDO V WEST HAM 08/01/2014
A quick look up and then a sumptuous curling shot that gave the Plzen keeper no chance from 25 yards, this goal was typical of Yaya Toure's superb season.	When Aleksandar Kolarov's cross was drilled into the United box, Sergio Aguero had to slightly adjust his run – and how – as he volleyed acrobatically in mid-air to give David de Gea no chance.	In red-hot form, Negredo controlled a long pass forward before controlling the ball, beating his man and rifling a powerful shot past Hugo Lloris from 20 yards for City's fifth goal of the afternoon.	City are blessed with several dead-ball specialists but none is deadlier than left-back Kolarov whose unerring accuracy from a distance was again evident as he blasted a 35-yard free-kick home away to Leicester.	One of the goals of this or any other season, Negredo's dart forward was spotted by Yaya Toure who lofted a superb 40-yard pass into the Spaniard's pass and without having to adjust his stride, Negredo volleyed home a low shot on the run. Stunning.

We've picked 10 crackers from the 2013/14 campaign – a season where City fans were spoilt for choice during a campaign where City scored more than 150 goals in all competitions. Here's ten of the best…

   04 **02**

YAYA V SUNDERLAND
02/03/2014

NASRI V SUNDERLAND
02/03/2014

SILVA V HULL CITY
15/03/2014

YAYA TOURE V FULHAM
22/03/2014

YAYA V ASTON VILLA
07/05/2014

Cometh the hour, cometh the man. As City tried to get back into the Capital One Cup final against Sunderland, the ball found its way to Yaya Toure who took a swing from 35 yards that gave the keeper no chance. A stunning goal.

With City fans still celebrating the Yaya Toure goal in the Capital One Cup final, Kolarov ran down the left, crossed the ball low into the box where Nasri ran at full pelt to curl the ball home with a superb right-foot shot – cue wild scenes at Wembley!

City, down to ten men and with their backs to the wall, needed a flash of brilliance to edge ahead away to Hull – Silva provided it as he traded passes with Yaya Toure before running towards the left of the Tigers' box and unleashing a sublime curling shot to put the Blues ahead.

A penalty, a free-kick and a stunning shot from 30 yards completed Yaya's hat-trick against Fulham – it was the latter that makes it into our Top 10 list.

Though Yaya could have had a Top 10 list of his own, this solo effort had to be included in our Goal of the Season collection. Picking the ball up deep in his own half, Yaya powered forward and just kept going, leaving defenders in his wake before powering the ball home to make it 4-0 against Villa.

Capital One Cup
Champions!

City won the Capital One Cup – formerly the League Cup – for the first time since 1976 when they beat Sunderland 3-1 at Wembley. Here are the teams City beat along the way and scorers...

And we're off...

The team lines up with the mascot of the day.

Samir Nasri is leapt upon by Edin Dzeko with the second.

Yaya scores the first of City's goals.

Jesus Navas wraps it up with a third - party time!

SEPTEMBER 24, 2013
Round 3: Wigan (H) 5-0
Dzeko 33, Jovetic 60,83, Yaya Toure 76,
Navas 86
Att: 25,519

OCTOBER 30, 2013
Round 4: Newcastle United (A) 2-0
Negredo 99, Dzeko 105
Att: 33,846

DECEMBER 17, 2013
Round 5: Leicester City (A) 3-1
Kolarov 8, Dzeko 41, 53
Att: 31,319

JANUARY 8, 2014
Semi-final, first leg: West Ham (H) 6-0
Negredo 12, 26, 49, Yaya Toure 40, Dzeko
60, 89

JANUARY 21, 2014
Semi-final, second leg: West Ham (A) 3-0
Negredo 3, 59 Aguero 24
(City win 9-0 on aggregate)
Att: 14,390

CAPITAL ONE CUP FINAL
March 2 (at Wembley): Sunderland 3-1
Yaya Toure 55, Nasri 56, Navas 90

Pablo Zabaleta and Alvero Negredo pose for the camera.

WINNERS 2014
Capital One Cup FINAL 2014

The players take to the podium to recieve the cup.

The coolest guvnor in football? - Manuel takes it all in his stride.

Jesus Navas and David Silva let the moment sink in.

Blue army!

Champions Parade

City toured the sun-drenched streets of Manchester on an open-top bus to parade the Premier League trophy and the Capital One Cup as more than 100,000 fans cheered, sang and waved as their heroes passed by. The pictures tell their own story...

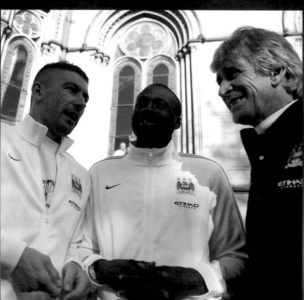

CHAMPIONS 2014

Training Ground
funnies There's a lot of hard work on the training ground, but plenty of fun, too...

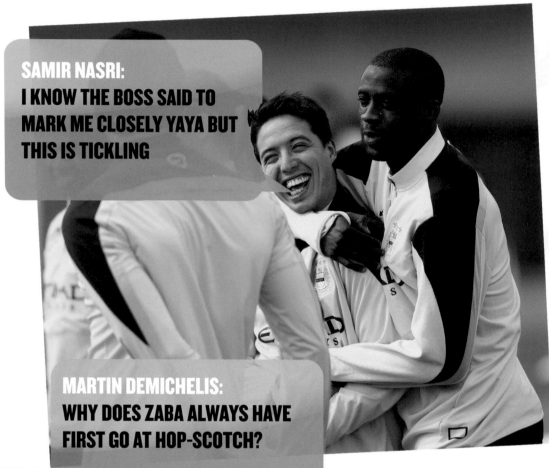

SAMIR NASRI:
I KNOW THE BOSS SAID TO MARK ME CLOSELY YAYA BUT THIS IS TICKLING

MARTIN DEMICHELIS:
WHY DOES ZABA ALWAYS HAVE FIRST GO AT HOP-SCOTCH?

Who's Celebrating?

Can you work out who is celebrating for City? We've disguised the image but see if you can figure out who the mystery player is?

Answer on page 60&61

Wordsearch#1

Find the words in the grid. Words can go horizontally, vertically and diagonally in all eight directions.

```
F F K O L A R O V Z K K T
T T R A H M S I L V A O C
O F M Y H C I L C F R M I
U S E D N R R D R E K P S
R A T R S D Z O U B F A A
E V T A N E O G D N N N T
Q A N E K A A D R W G Y S
P N L O L L N E E A E X A
G A O M T A N D R R B L N
M N P M B L B C I W G D L
T G E J I G I A M N N E K
P A S M K A P W Z B H V N
M S C I T E V O J H K O P
```

Aguero Clichy Dzeko Fernandinho Garcia Hart Jovetic
Kolarov Kompany Lopes Milner Nasri Nastasic Navas
Negredo Rodwell Sagna Silva Toure Zabaleta

Answers on page 60&61

Name Game#1

**We've disguised four City players below
- but who are they?**

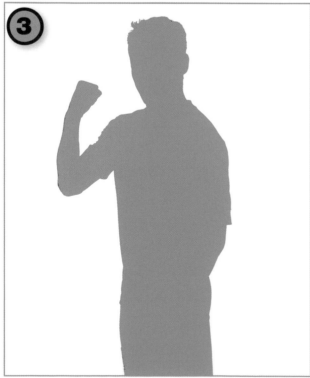

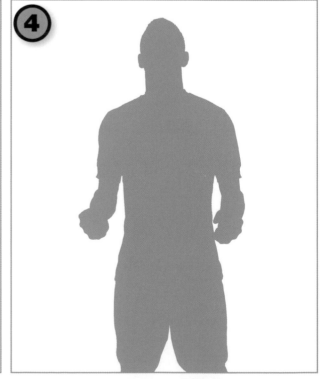

Answers on page 60&61

FERNANDO

SERGIO AGUERO

Some facts, figures and trivia on our Argentine superstar…
Born on 2 June 1988 in the rural community of Quilmes,
Sergio Leonel Aguero Del Castillo, Sergio used the bumpy
waste ground around the family home to practice his dribbling
skills and it was soon evident he had a very special talent.

Facts & Trivia

Sergio has a massive following on Twitter – 6,500,000 by the end of July 2014.

Sergio signed for his boyhood idols Independiente at the age of nine and he was just 15 years and 35 days old when he made his debut – the youngest in the club's history.

His family nicknamed him 'Kun' because he resembled a cartoon character called 'Kum-Kum' – today Sergio uses Kun as part of his shirt name.

Sergio made his debut for Argentina in 2006 against Brazil and up to the end of the 2014 World Cup, he'd won 54 caps and scored 21 goals.

By the end of the 2013/14 campaign, Kun had scored 75 goals in just 122 games for City and his overall career record at club and international level was 412 appearances and 199 goals.

Sergio's son Benjamin has true footballing gold in his DNA – his grandfather is Diego Maradona, considered one of the greatest footballers of all time.

Sergio won an Olympic Gold medal when Argentina won the 2008 football tournament.

Sergio's international room-mate is Lionel Messi.

Individual: Honours

2007: Golden Boot for top goalscorer (6 goals) of the U-20 World Cup (4th Argentinean player to achieve it after Ramon Diaz, 1979, Javier Saviola, 2001 and Lionel Messi, 2005).

2007: Golden Ball for U-20 World Cup Player of the Tournament (4th Argentinean player to achieve it after Diego Maradona, 1979, Javier Saviola, 2001 and Lionel Messi, 2005).

2005: Clar n Revelación de Oro Award for Breakthrough Player of the Year (shared with Lionel Messi).

2007: Fourth player in history to obtain both the Golden Ball and Golden Boot on the same U-20 competition (along with Geovani in 1983 for Brazil, and Javier Saviola in 2001 and Lionel Messi in 2005 for Argentina).

2007-2008: Antonio Puerta Trophy to best player in Spanish First Division, sponsored by Canal+.

2007: Tuttosport Golden Boy Award to best U-21 European player.

2007-2008: EFE Trophy to best Ibero-American player in Spanish First Division.

2007-2008: Second place on Alfredo Di Stefano Award to best Spanish First Division player, sponsored by Spanish newspaper Marca.

"IN MY CAREER SO FAR IT'S THE MOST IMPORTANT GOAL. YOU SCORE THE GOAL IN THE LAST MINUTE TO WIN THE TITLE. YOU'RE NOT SURE IF THAT'S EVER GOING TO HAPPEN IN YOUR CAREER AGAIN. I WISH I COULD TELL YOU HOW I DID IT BUT I CAN'T. I THOUGHT FOR ALL THE WORLD THAT MARIO BALOTELLI WAS GOING TO HAVE A GO HIMSELF BUT HE JUST MOVED IT ON ONE MORE AND IT FELL AT MY FEET AND I JUST THOUGHT: 'HIT THE TARGET, HIT IT AS HARD AS YOU CAN AND HIT THE TARGET.' AND IT WENT IN."

2008: GQ Award for Sportsman of the Year.

2008: Comunidad Iberoamericana Trophy for most outstanding performance of an n Ibero-American sportsman of 2008.

2011-2012: Man City's Player of the Year Honours

Name Game#2

Fill in the box below with the letters indicated from the questions below...

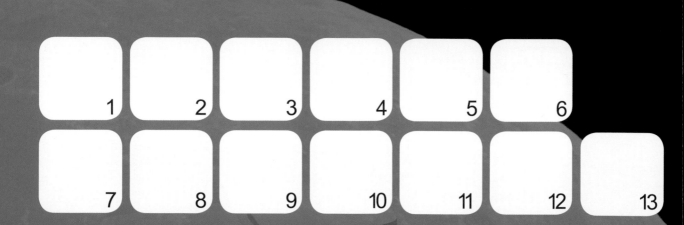

1	2	3	4	5	6

7	8	9	10	11	12	13

6 & 7:   Initials of the player they call The Magician.

1 & 10:   Initials of City's Bosnian Diamond.

13 & 12:   Initials of City's biggest rivals!

2 & 4:   Initials of a London team City beat 6-0 at home and 5-1 away in 2013/14.

5 & 9:   Second and fourth letters of Mr Toure's first name.

3:     Final letter of Garcia's first name.

11 & 8:   Second and third letters of the name of the club, without the Manchester!

Answers on page 60&61

Kit Designer

Let's see how you fare at designing City's mythical 'fourth kit'...

Spot the Difference

David Silva is seeing double here, can you find the seven differences between the two pictures.

Answers on page 60&61

Who's Texting?

You can see it now – the phone vibrates and there's a text message. Who could the message be for? Try and work out from the clues below...

'Can't believe you went out in the group stages! Still, you've a World Cup winner's medal and a Euro 2012 winner's medal to go along with your two Premier League winner's medals!'

'Welcome to City! Great to have another Brazilian in the team but got to warn you, it's not as hot as it is in Portugal!'

'Just run out of shampoo – hoping you can help? Ha, ha!'

'Don't forget to ask Messi for a signed shirt on the next trip. I've asked Zaba but he forgot – hoping for better luck from his striker partner!'

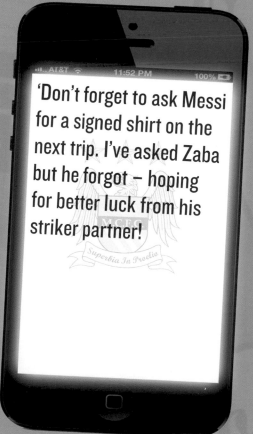

Answers on page 60&61

Crossword

Fill the puzzle by answering the clues below.

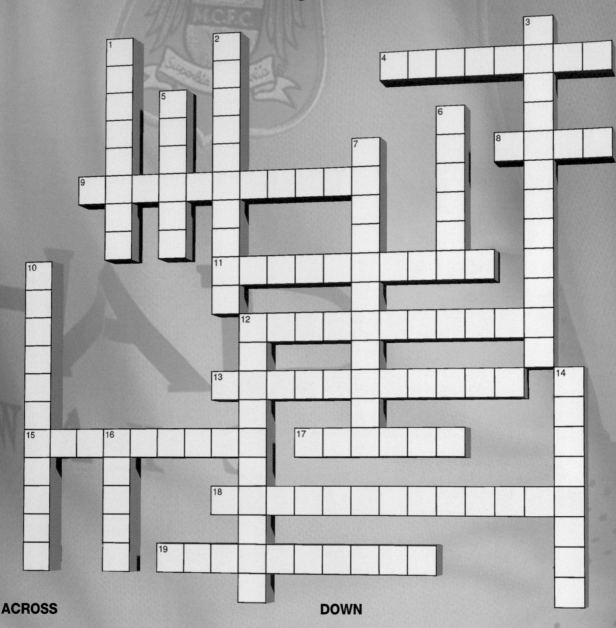

ACROSS

04 She's our mascot. (8)
08 Sports firm who make City's kit. (4)
09 He's our mascot. (11)
11 Yaya's home nation. (5,5)
12 Pellegrini's nickname. (3,8)
13 American sister club of City. (3,4,4)
15 Team who knocked City out of the 2013/14 Champions League. (9)
17 Country Fernandinho represents. (6)
18 Where City play their home games. (6,7)
19 Former Benfica and Real Madrid midfielder who plays for City. (4,6)

DOWN

01 Aleks Kolarov's lethal weapon. (4,4)
02 Martin, the Argentina defender. (10)
03 City's top scorer in 2013/14. (6,6)
05 Edin Dzeko's home nation. (6)
06 Joe Hart needs these to play. (6)
07 David Silva was born here. (4,7)
10 City player who spent all 2013/14 season with Everton. (6,5)
12 Vincent Kompany is this. (3,7)
14 City fans' theme song. (4,4)
16 Country Manuel Pellegrini was born in. (5)

Answers on page 60&61

STEVAN JOVETIC

THE BIG CITY QUIZ

01
Four City players reached the 20-goal mark in all competitions during the 2013/14 season – can you name them all? One point for each correct answer.

02
City's lowest combined tally for goals scored against one club home and away in the Premier League during the 2013/14 campaign is one – which two clubs managed to keep City out the most? One point for each club named.

03
Who scored the quickest goal of last season?

04
Who scored City's 100th goal in all competitions last season?

05
Who scored the Blues' 100th Premier League goal last season?

06
Can you name the four teams to win at the Etihad Stadium during the 2013/14 season (all competitions)? One point for each correct answer.

07
Which team did Manuel Pellegrini manage before City?

08
Who did City fans nickname 'The Beast'?

09
Which City player captained Montenegro against England at Wembley?

10
How many times did City score six or more goals last season in all competitions? One point for each club named.

11
Which landmark did Yaya Toure reach during the 2013/14 season?

12
Which City player scored in the Nou Camp against Barcelona?

13
In the FA Cup, which team did City have to come from 2-0 down against to win 4-2?

14
How many hat-tricks were scored during the 2013/14 season? 1 point for each 1 named.

15
Which City striker is known as 'The Diamond'?

16
Which Arsenal player became City's first signing of the 2014/15 season?

How is your City knowledge? Think you have what it takes to take on The Big City Quiz? There are 50 points up for grabs – see how you get on and then see how you scored on our points table.

17
How many City players went to the World Cup in Brazil – and for one point each, can you name them all?

18
Which City player is nicknamed 'Merlin'?

19
Who does Marcos Lopes take his 'Ronny' nickname from?

20
Who scored an own goal for City in the 3-2 defeat at Liverpool?

21
Which two players scored against Manchester United both at home and away? One point for each correct answer.

22
Which team did Costel Pantilimon join after leaving City and how many times did he play against them last season?

23
Who scored in City's first and last Premier League games during the 2013/14 season?

24
Who scored City's extra time Capital One Cup goals at Newcastle? One point for each correct answer.

SCORE CHART:

50 - 40 points:
You know your stuff
– a champion in fact! Put the captain's armband on.

39 – 30:
Excellent work
– you're the Pablo Zabaleta of City quizzes!

29 – 20:
Not bad at all
– the equivalent of reaching the FA Cup quarter-finals and finishing sixth in the Premier League table.

19 - 10:
Decent effort
– the board have given you a vote of confidence!

Less than 10 points:
Oh dear!
– You're in relegation trouble and the chairman wants a word!

Answers on page 60&61

New Signing#1
WILLY CABALLERO

Argentinian goalkeeper Willy Caballero became City's third signing of the summer when he joined the Champions from Manuel Pellegrini's former club Malaga.

The 32-year-old will bring a wealth of experience as he joins fellow keepers Joe Hart and Richard Wright in a goalkeeping trio that is a match for any Premier League club.

Caballero began his career in his homeland with Boca Juniors, where he won the Argentine Primera League, Copa Libertadores and Intercontinental Cup in 2003. He then moved to Spain in 2004 and spent seven years with Elche, before linking up with Pellegrini at Malaga.

Caballero can't wait to challenge Hart for the No.1 jersey and shortly after arriving, he said: "I am very happy, and really looking forward to the start of pre-season and performing well to help the team.

"This is a new challenge and a new league for me. I have been doing well in the previous years and my goal is to go on and hopefully perform at the same level for City.

"I know I am coming to a big club with a very good goalkeeper. City already have a great goalkeeper in Joe Hart, but I will try and compete for the no.1 spot. I will do my best in the training sessions.

"The most beautiful moments of my career were under Manuel Pellegrini in Malaga, where we achieved big things and we made Malaga's name known around Europe. But I also like the way he works, I think his best quality is giving players the confidence to achieve their potential.

"As for my new Argentine team-mates, I have a very good relationship with Martin Demichelis, but prior to joining City, I had never met Pablo Zabaleta and Sergio Aguero. I'm looking forward to working with them on a daily basis. For me it is very good to have people from Argentina in the squad because I think it will be very helpful.

"I spoke to Roque Santa Cruz and Demichelis, and they told me that Manchester is a very beautiful city and very welcoming, so that will be great for my family and I can't wait to enjoy it."

Caballero won the U20 FIFA World Cup with Argentina in 2001, and was part of the squad that triumphed at the 2004 Summer Olympics as a 22-year-old, but the Premier League represents a new challenge for the Santa Elena-born stopper.

"I've always loved the Premier League, I watched it as a child and I always liked the style of play here," he said. "When I was 19 I came to play a friendly against England and I really liked how they played and how passionate the fans are. It's a big step in my career and a dream realised to play in the Premier League.

"Roque and Martin told me that the City fans are fantastic and that they are very supportive. Hopefully we can have many happy times together."

Name: Wilfredo Daniel Caballero Lazcano
Squad number: 13
Date of birth: 28 September 1981
Place of birth: Santa Elena, Argentina
Previous clubs: Boca Juniors, Elche, Arsenal Sarandi (loan), Malaga
Height: 6' 1"
International caps: 0

WorldCupCity

Here's how our players performed at the World Cup....

Joe Hart (England):
Played: 2 Won: 0 Drawn: 0
Lost: 2 Conceded: 4

Not a great tournament for Joe who was rarely called upon and couldn't do much about the goals that were scored against him. He will have been disappointed to have been beaten by two headers and an effort from long range.

James Milner (England):
Played: 1 Won: 0 Drawn: 1
Lost: 0 Goals: 0

Unused in the first two matches, James Milner was only given a chance in the final game against Costa Rica where he gave his usual all-action performance and was one of England's better players.

Edin Dzeko (Bosnia):
Played: 3 Won: 1 Drawn: 0
Lost: 2 Goals: 1

Edin can consider himself unlucky not to have had a better tournament than he actually had. He had a perfectly good goal against Nigeria ruled out for offside – a game Bosnia eventually lost 1-0, but at least found the net in the final game, a 3-1 win over Iran.

David Silva (Spain):
Played: 3 Won: 1 Drawn: 0
Lost: 2 Goals: 0

Spain's exit from the World Cup at the group stage was one of the shocks of the World Cup. A thrashing by Holland and then Chile saw La Roja out after two games with a 3-0 win over Australia the only victory.

Yaya Toure (Ivory Coast):
Played: 3 Won: 1 Drawn: 0
Lost: 2 Goals: 0

Despite starting with a 2-1 win over Japan, Yaya's Ivory Coast lost their next two games to go out at the group stages. Yaya was perhaps not fully fit but The Elephants will no doubt have been disappointed not to progress having lost their final game to a last-minute penalty to Greece.

Bacary Sagna (France):
Played: 1 Won: 0 Drawn: 1
Lost: 0 Goals: 0

He started the tournament officially as an Arsenal player but ended as a City player – but Bacary Sagna was only used in the 0-0 draw against Ecuador. France reached the quarter-finals, but Sagna was an unused sub in four matches for Les Bleus.

Vincent Kompany (Belgium):
Played: 5 Won: 4 Drawn: 0
Lost: 1 Goals: 0

City's Captain Fantastic almost led Belgium to glory but the Red Devils lost 1-0 to Argentina in the quarter-finals. At his commanding best throughout the tournament, he could do little about the winning goal for Argentina in the last eight.

Fernandinho (Brazil):
Played: 4 Won: 3 Drawn: 0
Lost: 1 Goals: 1

Though Fernandinho was unused in the first two Brazil matches, when he was brought in for the final group game, he made an instant impact by assisting one goal and scoring another. He then became an integral part in Brazil's World Cup bid playing the sort of football he had all season for City as the hosts reached the semi-final, but he – and the entire team – were well below their best as Germany thrashed Brazil 7-1.

Martin Demichelis (Argentina):
Played: 1 Won: 1 Drawn: 0
Lost: 0 Goals: 0

Unused in the first four Argentina matches, Martin Demichelis came in for his first game during the quarter-final victory over Belgium. Having been absent for three years, his form at City won him a surprise call-up for the World Cup squad and he was excellent when he was finally called upon.

Sergio Aguero (Argentina):
Played: 3 Won: 3 Drawn: 0
Lost: 0 Goals: 0

Injury curtailed Sergio Aguero's World Cup when he had to limp off against Nigeria in the final group game. Though not at his best, he was always lively and a threat but carried the problems that had plagued the 2013/14 season into the Brazil 2014 tournament.

Pablo Zabaleta (Argentina):
Played: 5 Won: 5 Drawn: 0
Lost: 0 Goals: 0

City's Mr Dependable was Argentina's Mr Reliable during the World Cup where he played every match and minute of Argentina's World Cup campaign. Solid at the back and a genuine attacking threat down the right flank, Zaba was one of the unsung heroes of the competition.

WIN A SIGNED CITY 2014/15 HOME SHIRT!

Fancy owning a new City shirt signed by all your favourite players?

Answer the following question to be in with a chance:
What was City's former home called?

A) Maine Road
B) Main Road
C) Main Way

Entry is by email only. One entry per contestant. Please enter MCFC SHIRT followed by either A, B or C in the subject line of an email. In the body of the email, please include your name, address, postcode, email address and phone number and send to: frontdesk@grangecommunications.co.uk by Friday 27 March 2015.

Competition Terms and Conditions

Entry is by email only. Only one entry per contestant. Please enter MCFC SHIRT followed by either A, B or C in the subject line of an email. In the body of the email, please include your full name, address, postcode, email address and phone number and send to: frontdesk@grangecommunications.co.uk by Friday 27 March 2015.

1) The closing date for this competition is Friday 27th March 2015 at midnight. Entries received after that time will not be counted.

2) Information on how to enter and on the prize form part of these conditions.

3) Entry is open to those residing in the UK only. If entrants are under 18, consent from a parent or guardian must be obtained and the parent or guardian must agree to these terms and conditions. If entrants are under 13, this consent must be given in writing from the parent or guardian with their full contact details.

4) This competition is not open to employees or their relatives of Manchester City Football Club. Any such entries will be invalid.

5) The start date for entries is 31st October 2014 at 4pm.

6) Entries must be strictly in accordance with these terms and conditions. Any entry not in strict accordance with these terms and conditions will be deemed to be invalid and no prize will be awarded in respect of such entry. By entering, all entrants will be deemed to accept these rules.

7) One (1) lucky winner will win a 2014/15 season signed football shirt.

8) The prize is non-transferable and no cash alternative will be offered. Entry is by email only. Only one entry per contestant. Please enter MCFC SHIRT followed by either A, B or C in the subject line of an email. In the body of the email, please include your full name, address, postcode, email address and phone number and send to: frontdesk@grangecommunications.co.uk by Friday 27 March 2015.

9) The winner will be picked at random. The winner will be contacted within 72 hours of the closing date. Details of the winner can be requested after this time from the address below.

10) Entries must not be sent in through agents or third parties. No responsibility can be accepted for lost, delayed, incomplete, or for electronic entries or winning notifications that are not received or delivered. Any such entries will be deemed void.

11) The winner will have 72 hours to claim their prize once initial contact has been made by the Promoter. Failure to respond may result in forfeiture of the prize.

12) On entering the competition you are allowing Manchester City Football Club to contact you with information about products and services they believe might be of interest to you. If you do not wish to receive any marketing information from the Club, you can opt out at any time by emailing MCFC STOP to frontdesk@grangecommunications.co.uk. Your information will always be safeguarded under the terms and conditions of the Data Protection Act 1998 and MCFC's Privacy Policy (http://www.mcfc.co.uk/Common/Privacy) to ensure that the information you provide is safe.

13) The Promoter reserves the right to withdraw or amend the promotion as necessary due to circumstances outside its reasonable control. The Promoter's decision on all matters is final and no correspondence will be entered into.

14) The Promoter (or any third party nominated by the Promoter) may use the winner's name and image and their comments relating to the prize for future promotional, marketing and publicity purposes in any media worldwide without notice and without any fee being paid.

15) This competition shall be governed by English law.

16) Promoter: Grange Communications Ltd, 22 Great King Street, Edinburgh EH3 6QH. Any questions relating to this competition should be referred to the Promoter and not to MCFC.

LOAN SIGNING:
Frank Lampard

Frank Lampard joined City for the start of the 2014/15 season. The England midfielder had left Chelsea over the summer and joined City's MLS side New York City FC on a two-year deal, but under league rules, he was eligible to be loaned to City for six months.

The deal will allow Lampard to continue playing in the Premier League before he begins a new life in the USA and in turn, he will bring a wealth of experience with him to City. Lampard played 648 times for Chelsea and scored a record 211 goals – not bad for a midfielder and a record that made him a legend at Stamford Bridge. The former England skipper has also won 106 caps for his country to date and intends to still be available for Roy Hodgson's squad when he begins the qualification process for the Euro 2016 tournament over the next two years. Though 36, Lampard is expected to add vital know-how to the Blues' Champions League bid this season having won the competition with Chelsea in 2012 and the three-times Premier League winner will also aim to help City to another title success during his stay at the Etihad Stadium. Frank will wear the No.18 shirt this season.

JESUS NAVAS

Wordsearch#2

Find the words in the grid. Words can go horizontally, vertically and diagonally in all eight directions.

```
C Q N A M S D N U O R G E S P
D C R O W D F K G S X C R L S
J R N Q W C M O G F I E V D N
S Q L P T V A O P L G M R S M
S N L V I L D Q O A B A R E U
C V A D S T W P N Z W E T V I
O I B F O X C A W E F E X R D
R S T H Y B M H T E W M T A A
E R O Y P A Y S R L K M I C T
B E O T S X W E W P D A C S S
O Y F L M Q E A G F B R K N R
A A D B V C U N M L H G E W C
R L C A M E R A M A N O T D N
D P Q V V D D T R Q T R S Y B
Q Y O B L L A B Z E V P T M B
```

AwayFans Ballboy Cameraman CitySquare Crowd Football Goals Groundsman HotDogs Managers Pitch Players Police Programme Referee Scarves Scoreboard Stadium Stewards Tickets

Answers on page 60&61

New Signing#2
FERNANDO FRANCISCO REGES

Fernando Francisco Reges became City's second signing of the summer after joining City from Porto in June 2014. The Brazilian-born holding midfielder spent seven years in Portugal, lifting four Primeira Liga trophies during his time at the Estadio do Dragao.

Raised in the Brazilian suburb of Alto Paraíso-born, Fernando is a defensive midfielder with a wealth of UEFA Champions League experience having appeared in the competition with Porto champions in five of the last six seasons. A quick, rangy and explosive midfielder, recognised for his abilities to anticipate and break up opposition attack, Fernando will complement Fernandinho, Yaya Toure and Javi Garcia in the holding midfield role within the team.

He began his career in his homeland with Vila Nova Futebol Clube in the third tier of the Brazilian league, making his professional debut in 2005.

Snapped up by Porto after 57 league appearances, he was immediately loaned out for the following season to fellow Primeira Liga outfit, C.F. Estrala Amadora. After quickly adapting his style to European football, Fernando missed just four games all season and quickly became an integral member of the team.

Upon his return to Porto, he was immediately placed into the first-team and became a regular starter alongside Lucho González and Raul Meireles, helping Porto to a league and Portuguese Cup double in his first season.

In 2010/11, the Brazilian clocked up more than 3,000 minutes as Porto claimed a league, cup and Europa League treble under future Chelsea and Spurs boss Andre Villas Boas.

He started 14 times in the Europa League that season, including the final in Dublin against Braga, where he lined up alongside compatriots Helton and Hulk. The then-23-year old also played against City in both legs of the last 32 clash of the same competition in the following season, when City ended Porto's title defence with a 6-1 aggregate win.

However, Fernando would end that 2011/12 season by lifting the Portuguese league trophy – a feat he repeated for the fourth time the following season.

Virtually ever-present during the 2013/14 campaign, the midfielder missed just five league games all season and played every minute of the Portuguese side's Champions League campaign.

In total, Fernando played for Porto 232 times and scored five goals and the 26-year old will be hoping to expand on his impressive collection of titles as a City player, which already includes the UEFA Europa League (x1) the Portuguese League (x4) the Portuguese Cup (x2) and the Portuguese Supercup (x5).

Like compatriot Fernandinho, he also hopes moving to City will lead to international recognition with Brazil

Position: Midfielder
Squad number: No. 6
Date of birth: 25 July 1988
Place of birth: Alto Paraiso, Brazil
Height: 6'0"
International caps/goals: 3/0
(Brazil Under-20s)

New Signing#3
BACARY SAGNA

Bacary Sagna's signing was announced just before the 2014 World Cup in Brazil with the France defender agreeing to join the Blues from Arsenal on a three-year deal.
The 31-year-old brings with him a wealth of international and Champions League experience and will provide stiff competition for right-back Pablo Zabaleta, though Sagna is happy to play in central defence as and when needed.
So where did it all begin for Sagna?
His first club was FC Sens, but it was with Auxerre that the tough-tackling defender really caught the eye, playing 89 times for the Ligue 1 side and winning the French Cup with the Burgundy side. He won 12 France Under-21 caps.
Sagna left Auxerre in 2007, bringing an end to a nine-year association with the club. He hit the ground running at Arsenal and was named in the PFA Team of the Year in 2007/08 and achieved the feat again in 2010/11, but his only silverware came in 2014 when Arsenal beat Hull City in the FA Cup final.
His international career began in 2007 against Slovakia and he has so far won 41 caps for his country and was part of the 2014 Les Bleus World Cup squad.
Sagna made 284 appearances for Arsenal, assisted 22 goals, scored five and his final game was also the occasion he won his first piece of silverware as the Gunners beat Hull City in the 2014 FA Cup final.
Sagna also added another World Cup appearance to his bow by appearing for Les Bleus in Brazil 2014 after also appearing in the 2010 tournament in South Africa. He would no doubt have added many more caps to his 42 to date had he not suffered a broken leg prior to the 2012 European Championships.
Bacary's no-nonsense defending is certain to make him a popular figure among the City fans.

Position: Defender
Squad number: No. 3
Date of birth: 14 February 1983
Place of birth: Sens, France
Previous clubs: FC Sens, Auxerre, Arsenal
Height: 5'09"
International caps goals: 42/0

NAME:
JOE HART
POSITION:
GOALKEEPER
SQUAD NUMBER:
1

HART

Date of Birth:
19/04/1987

Previous Clubs:
Shrewsbury, Tranmere
Rovers (loan),
Blackpool (loan),
Birmingham City (loan)

**2013/14 Apps
(All Comps):**
39 starts

**2013/14 Goals
(All Comps):**
0

TOTAL CITY CAREER:

Played:
256

Goals:
0

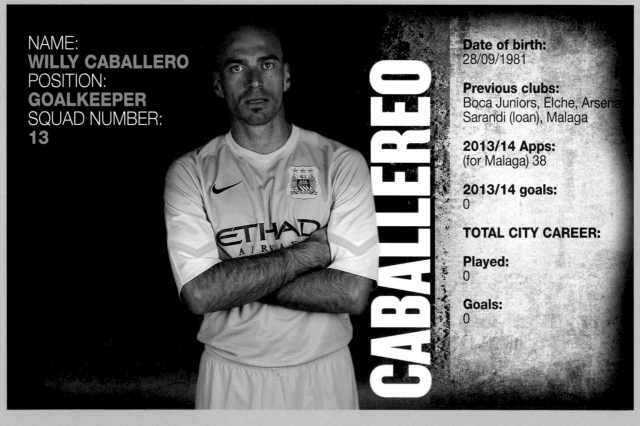

NAME:
WILLY CABALLERO
POSITION:
GOALKEEPER
SQUAD NUMBER:
13

CABALLERO

Date of birth:
28/09/1981

Previous clubs:
Boca Juniors, Elche, Arsenal
Sarandi (loan), Malaga

2013/14 Apps:
(for Malaga) 38

2013/14 goals:
0

TOTAL CITY CAREER:

Played:
0

Goals:
0

NAME:
GAEL CLICHY
POSITION:
LEFT-BACK
SQUAD NUMBER:
22

CLICHY

Date of Birth:
26/07/1985

Previous Clubs:
Cannes, Arsenal

**2013/14 Apps
(All Comps):**
28 starts, 3 sub

**2012/13 Goals
(All Comps):**
0

TOTAL CITY CAREER:

Played:
96 (9)

Goals:
1

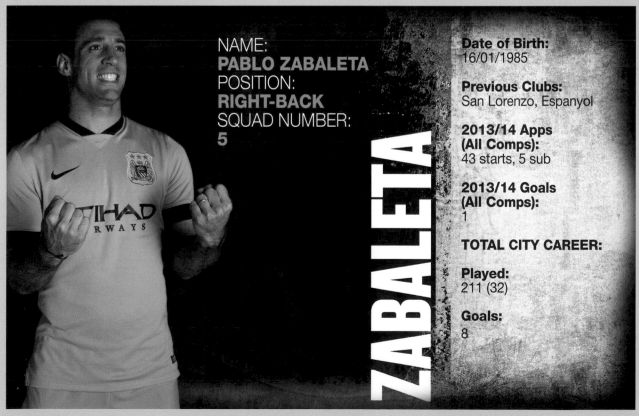

NAME:
PABLO ZABALETA
POSITION:
RIGHT-BACK
SQUAD NUMBER:
5

ZABALETA

Date of Birth:
16/01/1985

Previous Clubs:
San Lorenzo, Espanyol

**2013/14 Apps
(All Comps):**
43 starts, 5 sub

**2013/14 Goals
(All Comps):**
1

TOTAL CITY CAREER:

Played:
211 (32)

Goals:
8

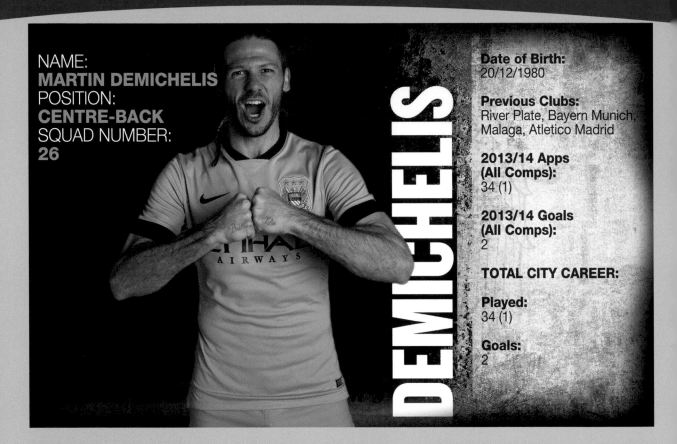

NAME:
MARTIN DEMICHELIS
POSITION:
CENTRE-BACK
SQUAD NUMBER:
26

DEMICHELIS

Date of Birth:
20/12/1980

Previous Clubs:
River Plate, Bayern Munich, Malaga, Atletico Madrid

2013/14 Apps (All Comps):
34 (1)

2013/14 Goals (All Comps):
2

TOTAL CITY CAREER:

Played:
34 (1)

Goals:
2

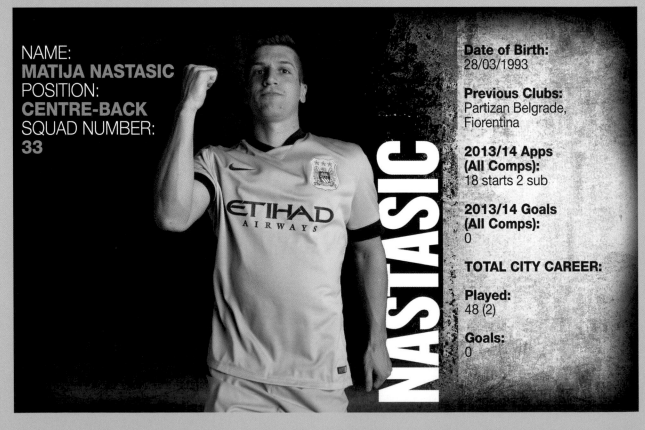

NAME:
MATIJA NASTASIC
POSITION:
CENTRE-BACK
SQUAD NUMBER:
33

NASTASIC

Date of Birth:
28/03/1993

Previous Clubs:
Partizan Belgrade, Fiorentina

2013/14 Apps (All Comps):
18 starts 2 sub

2013/14 Goals (All Comps):
0

TOTAL CITY CAREER:

Played:
48 (2)

Goals:
0

NAME:
VINCENT KOMPANY
(CAPTAIN)
POSITION:
CENTRE-BACK
SQUAD NUMBER:
4

KOMPANY

Date of Birth:
10/04/1986

Previous Clubs:
Anderlecht, SV Hamburg

**2013/14 Apps
(All Comps):**
36 starts 1 sub

**2012/13 Goals
(All Comps):**
5

TOTAL CITY CAREER:

Played:
234 (9)

Goals:
12

NAME:
DEDRYCK BOYATA
POSITION:
DEFENDER
SQUAD NUMBER:
38

BOYATA

Date of Birth:
26/11/1990

Previous Clubs:
Bolton Wanderers (loan),
FC Twente (loan)

**2013/14 Apps
(All Comps):**
5 starts, 1 sub

**2013/14 Goals
(All Comps):**
0

TOTAL CITY CAREER:

Played:
21 (9)

Goals:
1

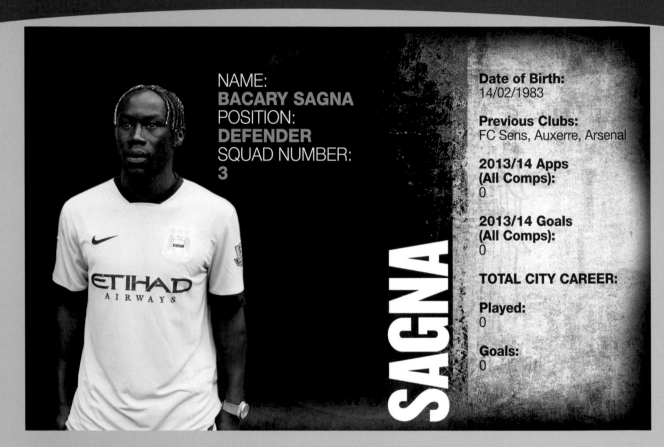

NAME:
BACARY SAGNA
POSITION:
DEFENDER
SQUAD NUMBER:
3

SAGNA

Date of Birth:
14/02/1983

Previous Clubs:
FC Sens, Auxerre, Arsenal

**2013/14 Apps
(All Comps):**
0

**2013/14 Goals
(All Comps):**
0

TOTAL CITY CAREER:

Played:
0

Goals:
0

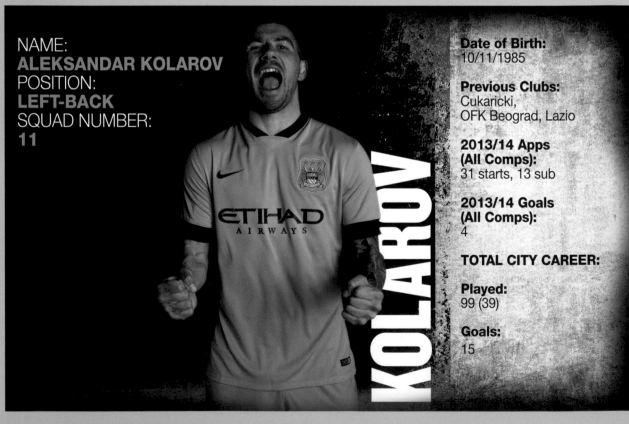

NAME:
ALEKSANDAR KOLAROV
POSITION:
LEFT-BACK
SQUAD NUMBER:
11

KOLAROV

Date of Birth:
10/11/1985

Previous Clubs:
Cukaricki,
OFK Beograd, Lazio

**2013/14 Apps
(All Comps):**
31 starts, 13 sub

**2013/14 Goals
(All Comps):**
4

TOTAL CITY CAREER:

Played:
99 (39)

Goals:
15

NAME:
ELIAQUIM MANGALA
POSITION:
DEFENDER
SQUAD NUMBER:
20

MANGALA

Date of Birth:
13 February 1991

Previous Clubs:
Standard Liege, Porto

**2013/14 Apps
(All Comps):**
42 apps 5 goals (for Porto)

**2013/14 Goals
(All Comps):**

TOTAL CITY CAREER:

Played:
0

Goals:
0

NAME:
JAMES MILNER
POSITION:
**MIDFIELD (LEFT,
RIGHT, CENTRE)**
SQUAD NUMBER:
7

MILNER

Date of Birth:
04/01/1986

Previous Clubs:
Leeds United, Swindon
Town (loan), Newcastle
United, Aston Villa

**2013/14 Apps
(All Comps):**
21 starts, 22 sub

**2013/14 Goals
(All Comps):**
2

TOTAL CITY CAREER:

Played:
99 (58)

Goals:
10

NAME:
FERNANDO
POSITION:
MIDFIELD
SQUAD NUMBER:
6

FERNANDO

Date of Birth:
25 July 1987

Previous Clubs:
Vila Nova, Estrela Amadora (loan), Porto

2013/14 Apps (All Comps):
36 apps 0 goals (for Porto)
Total City career: 0

2013/14 Goals (All Comps):
0

TOTAL CITY CAREER:

Played:
0

Goals:
0

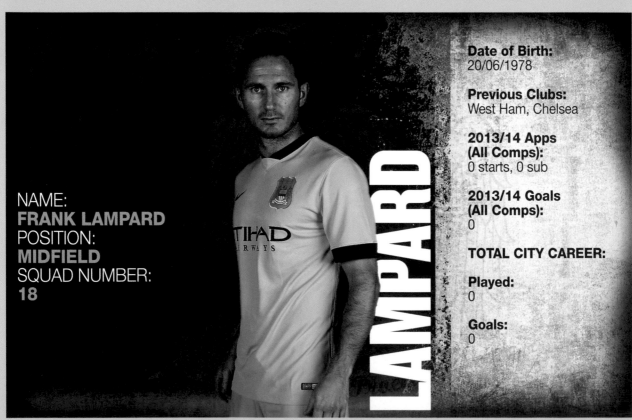

NAME:
FRANK LAMPARD
POSITION:
MIDFIELD
SQUAD NUMBER:
18

LAMPARD

Date of Birth:
20/06/1978

Previous Clubs:
West Ham, Chelsea

2013/14 Apps (All Comps):
0 starts, 0 sub

2013/14 Goals (All Comps):
0

TOTAL CITY CAREER:

Played:
0

Goals:
0

NAME:
JESUS NAVAS
POSITION:
ATTACKING MIDFIELD
SQUAD NUMBER:
15

NAVAS

Date of Birth:
21/11/1985

Previous Clubs:
Sevilla B, Sevilla

2013/14 Apps (All Comps):
29 starts, 19 sub

2013/14 Goals (All Comps):
6

TOTAL CITY CAREER:

Played:
29 (19)

Goals:
6

FERNANDINHO

NAME:
FERNANDINHO
POSITION:
MIDFIELD
SQUAD NUMBER:
25

Date of Birth:
04/05/1985

Previous Clubs:
Atletico Paranaense

2013/14 Apps (All Comps):
42 starts, 3 sub

2013/14 Goals (All Comps):
5

TOTAL CITY CAREER:

Played:
42 (3)

Goals:
5

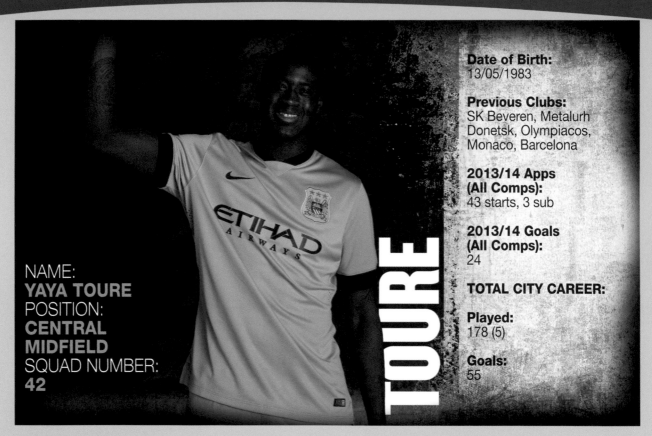

Date of Birth:
13/05/1983

Previous Clubs:
SK Beveren, Metalurh Donetsk, Olympiacos, Monaco, Barcelona

2013/14 Apps (All Comps):
43 starts, 3 sub

2013/14 Goals (All Comps):
24

TOTAL CITY CAREER:

Played:
178 (5)

Goals:
55

NAME:
YAYA TOURE
POSITION:
CENTRAL MIDFIELD
SQUAD NUMBER:
42

TOURE

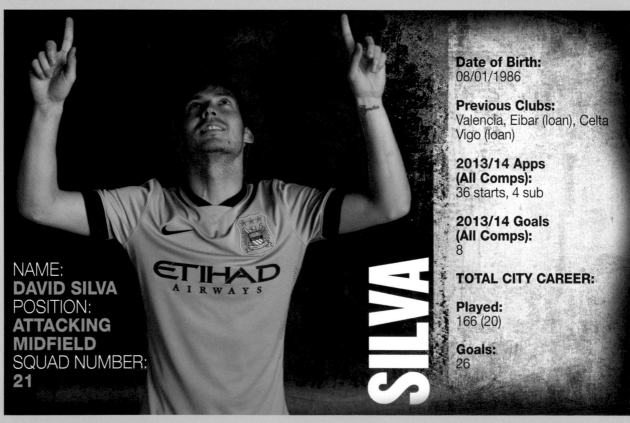

Date of Birth:
08/01/1986

Previous Clubs:
Valencia, Eibar (loan), Celta Vigo (loan)

2013/14 Apps (All Comps):
36 starts, 4 sub

2013/14 Goals (All Comps):
8

TOTAL CITY CAREER:

Played:
166 (20)

Goals:
26

NAME:
DAVID SILVA
POSITION:
ATTACKING MIDFIELD
SQUAD NUMBER:
21

SILVA

NAME:
SAMIR NASRI
POSITION:
ATTACKING MIDFIELD
SQUAD NUMBER:
8

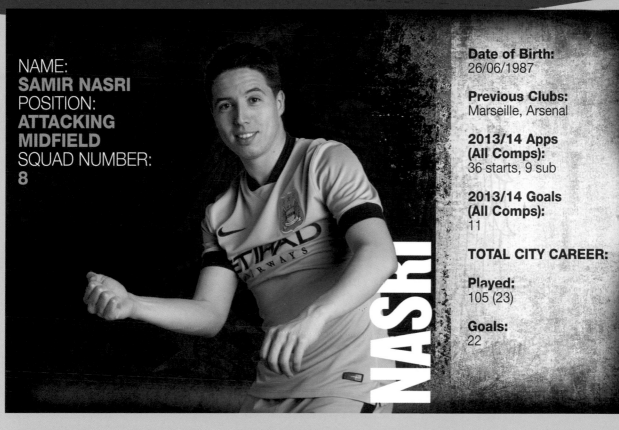

NASRI

Date of Birth:
26/06/1987

Previous Clubs:
Marseille, Arsenal

2013/14 Apps (All Comps):
36 starts, 9 sub

2013/14 Goals (All Comps):
11

TOTAL CITY CAREER:

Played:
105 (23)

Goals:
22

NAME:
STEVAN JOVETIC
POSITION:
STRIKER
SQUAD NUMBER:
35

JOVETIC

Date of Birth:
02/011/1989

Previous Clubs:
Partizan, Fiorentina

2013/14 Apps (All Comps):
5 starts, 13 sub

2013/14 Goals (All Comps):
6

TOTAL CITY CAREER:

Played:
9 (13)

Goals:
8

NAME:
SERGIO AGUERO
POSITION:
STRIKER
SQUAD NUMBER:
16

AGUERO

Date of Birth:
02/06/1988

Previous Clubs:
Independiente, Atlético Madrid

2013/14 Apps (All Comps):
30 starts, 4 sub

2012/13 Goals (All Comps):
28

TOTAL CITY CAREER:

Played:
99 (23)

Goals:
75

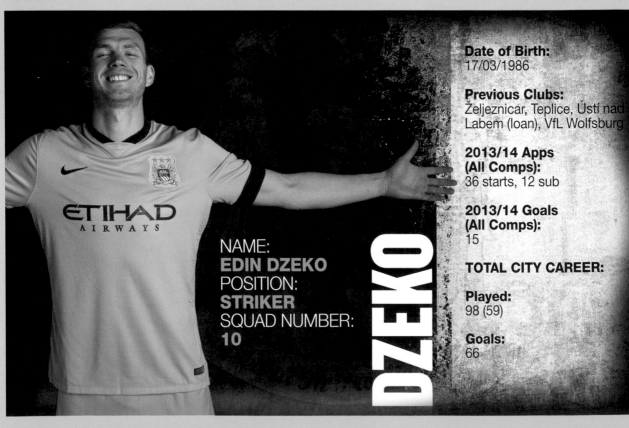

Date of Birth:
17/03/1986

Previous Clubs:
Željezničar, Teplice, Ústí nad Labem (loan), VfL Wolfsburg

2013/14 Apps (All Comps):
36 starts, 12 sub

2013/14 Goals (All Comps):
15

TOTAL CITY CAREER:

Played:
98 (59)

Goals:
66

NAME:
EDIN DZEKO
POSITION:
STRIKER
SQUAD NUMBER:
10

DZEKO

						F-A	Att	Pos	City scorers and goal times
1	Aug	Mon	19	H	Newcastle United	4-0	46,842	–	Silva 6, Aguero 22, Yaya Toure 50, Nasri 75
2		Sun	25	A	Cardiff City	2-3	27,068	6	Dzeko 52, Negredo 90
3		Sat	31	H	Hull City	2-0	46,903	3	Negredo 65, Yaya Toure 90
4	Sep	Sat	14	A	Stoke City	0-0	25,052	4	–
5		Tue	17	A	Viktoria Plzen (UEFA Champions League)	3-0	11,281	–	Dzeko 48, Yaya Toure 53, Aguero 58
6		Sun	22	H	Manchester United	4-1	47,156	3	Aguero 16, 47, Yaya Toure 45, Nasri 50
7		Tue	24	H	Wigan Athletic (Capital One Cup 3)	5-0	25,519	–	Dzeko 33, Jovetic 60, 83 Yaya Toure 76, Navas 86
8		Sat	28	A	Aston Villa	2-3	34,063	5	Yaya Toure 45, Dzeko 56
9	Oct	Wed	2	H	Bayern Munich (UEFA Champions League)	1-3	45,021	–	Negredo 79
10		Sat	5	H	Everton	3-1	47,267	5	Negredo 17, Aguero 45, Howard og 69
11		Sat	19	A	West Ham United	3-1	34,507	4	Aguero 16, 51, Silva 80
12		Wed	23	A	CSKA Moscow (UEFA Champions League)	2-1	14,000	–	Aguero 34, 42
13		Sun	27	A	Chelsea	1-2	41,495	7	Aguero 49
14		Wed	30	A	Newcastle United (Capital One Cup 4)	2-0	33,846	–	Negredo 99, Dzeko 105 (after extra-time)
15	Nov	Sat	2	H	Norwich City	7-0	47,066	4	Johnson og 16, Silva 20, Martin og 25, Negredo 36, Yaya Toure 60, Aguero 71, Dzeko 86
16		Tue	5	H	CSKA Moscow (UEFA Champions League)	5-2	38,512	–	Aguero pen 3, 20, Negredo 30, 51, 90+2
17		Sun	10	A	Sunderland	0-1	40,137	8	–
18		Sun	24	H	Tottenham Hotspur	6-0	47,227	4	Navas 1, 90+1, Sandro og 34, Aguero 41, 50, Negredo 55
19		Wed	27	H	Viktoria Plzen (UEFA Champions League)	4-2	37,712	–	Aguero pen 33, Nasri 65, Negredo 78, Dzeko 89
20	Dec	Sun	1	H	Swansea City	3-0	46,559	3	Negredo 8, Nasri 58, 77
21		Wed	4	A	West Bromwich Albion	3-2	22,943	3	Aguero 9, Yaya Toure 24, pen 74
22		Sat	7	A	Southampton	1-1	31,229	4	Aguero 10
23		Tue	10	A	Bayern Munich (UEFA Champions League)	3-2	68,000	–	Silva 28, Kolarov pen 59, Milner 62
24		Sat	14	H	Arsenal	6-3	47,229	3	Aguero 14, Negredo 39, Fernandinho 50, 88, Silva 66, Yaya Toure pen 90
25		Tue	17	A	Leicester City (Capital One Cup 5)	3-1	31,319	–	Kolarov 8, Dzeko 41, 53
26		Sat	21	A	Fulham	4-2	25,509	2	Yaya Toure 23, Kompany 43, Jesus Navas 78, Milner 83
27		Thu	26	H	Liverpool	2-1	47,351	2	Kompany 31, Negredo 45+1
28		Sat	28	H	Crystal Palace	1-0	47,107	1	Dzeko 66
29	Jan	Wed	1	A	Swansea City	3-2	20,498	2	Fernandinho 14, Yaya Toure 58, Kolarov 66
30		Sat	4	A	Blackburn Rovers (FA Cup 3)	1-1	18,813	–	Negredo 45
31		Wed	8	H	West Ham United (Capital One Cup SF1)	6-0	30,381	–	Negredo 12, 26, 49, Yaya Toure 40, Dzeko 60, 89
32		Sun	12	A	Newcastle United	2-0	49,423	1	Dzeko 8, Negredo 90+5
33		Wed	15	H	Blackburn Rovers (FA Cup 3 Replay)	5-0	33,102	–	Negredo 45+1, 47, Dzeko 67, 79, Aguero 73
34		Sat	18	H	Cardiff City	4-2	47,213	2	Dzeko 14, Navas 33, Yaya Toure 76, Aguero 79
35		Tue	21	A	West Ham United (Capital One Cup SF2)	3-0	14,390	–	Negredo 3, 59, Aguero 24 (City win 9-0 on aggregate)
36		Sat	25	H	Watford (FA Cup 4)	4-2	46,514	–	Aguero 60, 79, 90+2, Kolarov 87
37		Wed	29	A	Tottenham Hotspur	5-1	36,071	1	Aguero 15, Yaya Toure pen 51, Dzeko 53, Jovetic 78, Kompany 89
38	Feb	Mon	3	H	Chelsea	0-1	47,364	2	–
39		Sat	8	A	Norwich City	0-0	26,832	3	–
40		Sat	15	H	Chelsea (FA Cup 5)	2-0	47,013	–	Jovetic 16, Nasri 67
41		Tue	18	H	Barcelona (UEFA Champions League R16/1)	0-2	46,030	–	–
42		Sat	22	H	Stoke City	1-0	47,038	3	Yaya Toure 70
43	Mar	Sun	2	N	Sunderland (Capital One Cup Final)	3-1	84,697	–	Yaya Toure 55, Nasri 56, Jesus Navas 90 (at Wembley)
44		Sun	9	H	Wigan Athletic (FA Cup 6)	1-2	46,824	–	Nasri 68
45		Wed	12	A	Barcelona (UEFA Champions League R16/2)	1-2	85,957	–	Kompany 89 (Barcelona win 4-1 on aggregate)
46		Sat	15	A	Hull City	2-0	24,895	2	Silva 14, Dzeko 90
47		Sat	22	H	Fulham	5-0	47,262	3	Yaya Toure pen 26, pen 54, 65, Fernandinho 84, Demichelis 88
48		Tue	25	A	Manchester United	3-0	75,203	2	Dzeko 1, 56, Yaya Toure 90
49		Sat	29	A	Arsenal	1-1	60,060	3	Silva 18
50	Apr	Sat	5	H	Southampton	4-1	47,009	3	Yaya Toure pen 3, Nasri 45+1, Dzeko 45+4, Jovetic 81
51		Sun	13	A	Liverpool	2-3	44,601	3	Silva 57, Johnson og 62
52		Wed	16	H	Sunderland	2-2	47,046	3	Fernandinho 2, Nasri 88
53		Mon	21	H	West Bromwich Albion	3-1	46,564	3	Zabaleta 3, Aguero 10, Demichelis 36
54		Sun	27	A	Crystal Palace	2-0	24,769	3	Dzeko 4, Yaya Toure 43
55	May	Sat	3	A	Everton	3-2	39,454	1	Aguero 22, Dzeko 43, 48
56		Wed	7	H	Aston Villa	4-0	47,023	1	Dzeko 64, 72, Jovetic 89, Yaya Toure 90+2
57		Sun	11	H	West Ham United	2-0	47,407	1	Nasri 39, Komany 49

QuizAnswers

WHO'S CELEBRATING?
(From page 22)

WORDSEARCH#1
(From page 23)

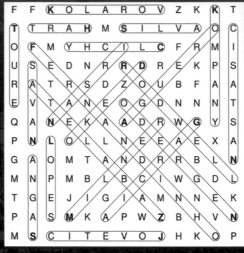

GUESS WHO?
(From page 24)

1 YAYA

2 KOMPANY

3 NAVAS

4 ZABALETA

SPOT THE DIFFERENCE?
(From page 30)

SHADES — **1**

2 NIKE SWOOSH

NECK COLLAR COLOUR — **3**

CREST-SHIELD BACKGROUND COLOUR — **4**

5 ARM COLLAR COLOUR

6 SHIRT MAKE LABEL

7 NIKE SWOOSH

WHO'S TEXTING?
(From page 31)

CAN'T BELIEVE YOU WENT OUT IN THE GROUP STAGES! STILL, YOU'VE A WOLRD CUP WINNER'S MEDAL AND A EURO 2012 WINNER'S MEDAL TO GO ALONG WITH YOUR TWO PREMIER LEAGUE WINNER'S MEDALS!'
(DAVID SILVA)

'WELCOME TO CITY! GREAT TO HAVE ANOTHER BRAZILIAN IN THE TEAM BUT GOT TO WARN YOU, IT'S NOT AS HOT AS IT IS IN PORTUGAL!'
(FERNANDO)

'JUST RUN OUT OF SHAMPOO – HOPING YOU CAN HELP? HA, HA!'
(JOE HART)

'DON'T FORGET TO ASK MESSI FOR A SIGNED SHIRT ON THE NEXT TRIP. I'VE ASKED ZABA BUT HE FORGOT – HOPING FOR BETTER LUCK FROM HIS STRIKER PARTNER!'
(SERGIO AGUERO)

NAME GAME
(From page 28)

6 & 7: D, S – DAVID SILVA
1 & 10: E, D – EDIN DZEKO
13 & 12: M, U – MAN UNITED
2 & 4: T, H - TOTTENHAM HOTSPUR
5 & 9: A, A – YAYA TOURE
3: I – A - JAVI GARCIA
11 & 8: I, T – CITY

SOLUTION:

ETIHAD STADIUM

THE BIG CITY QUIZ - ANSWERS
(From page 34&35)

1: AGUERO, TOURE, DZEKO, NEGREDO

2: CHELSEA, STOKE

3: NAVAS V SPURS

4: DZEKO

5: TOURE V VILLA

6: CHELSEA, BAYERN MUNICH, WIGAN, BARCELONA

7: MALAGA

8: ALVARO NEGREDO

9: STEVAN JOVETIC

10: FOUR TIMES - NORWICH/WEST HAM/SPURS/ ARSENAL

11: 50 GOALS FOR CITY

12: VINCENT KOMPANY

13: WATFORD

14: SEVILLA

15: FOUR - NEGREDO (CSKA), NEGREDO (WEST HAM), TOURE (FULHAM), AGUERO (WATFORD)

16: EDIN DZEKO

17: BACARY SAGNA

18: JOE HART, JAMES MILNER, DAVID SILVA, YAYA TOURE, EDIN DZEKO, SERGIO AGUERO, PABLO ZABALETA, MARTIN DEMICHELIS, VINCENT KOMPANY, FERNANDINHO

19: DAVID SILVA

20: CRISTIANO RONALDO

21: GLEN JOHNSON

22: DZEKO/TOURE

23: SUNDERLAND – HE PLAYED TWICE AGAINST THEM

24: SILVA FIRST/KOMPANY LAST

CROSSWORD
(From page 32)

WHERE'S PABLO?
(From page 62)

WORDSEARCH#2
(From page 43)

Where's Pablo?
Can you spot Pablo amidst the crowd?